Sarah Alexander.

Transformed Lives

Transformed Lives

How one ministry
is making a difference
around the world

Compiled by EDDIE TAIT
Foreword by SELWYN HUGHES

Contents

Foreword

Over the years it has been my privilege to see the lives of many people transformed through CWR's ministries. I am amazed, for example, at the ways in which passages I have written in *Every Day with Jesus* under the pressure of editorial deadlines have spoken deeply into people's situations – confirming, comforting, and encouraging. That's God at work! In our seminars we have seen people change as they have absorbed the truths of Scripture.

CWR's ministries, especially our counsellor training, have proved to be catalysts for the rise of many other ministries in this and related fields as our students have applied what they have learned on courses to their own lives and passed it on to others. Countless lives have been affected around the world. Truly we can say that 'the Lord has done this, and it is marvellous in our eyes' (Matt. 21:42).

This book contains vivid examples of how God has worked through CWR. The testimonies include one of a man who found Jesus through picking up *EDWJ* out of sheer boredom in a prison cell he had wrongfully been thrown into; of an Institute in Christian Counselling course giving a lady a vision to start a counselling centre that is now influencing many parts of Africa; of a singer/missionary who finds *EDWJ* keeps her close to the Lord in her travels; of a couple who started a successful youth ministry after an 'apprenticeship' at Waverley. There's a particularly moving testimony of being ministered to in the traumatic days following the murder of a daughter, while others tell of experiencing God's love and acceptance for who they are.

I commend each story to you, praying that you will be touched and blessed by the wonderful Lord whom we serve who has chosen us to be His instruments for the purpose of building His kingdom.

Selwyn Hughes
Founder and Director, CWR

LIGHT IN A PRISON CELL

Chris Wren

A Portuguese prison cell is one of the most unusual places where Every Day with Jesus *has been read and helped to transform the reader's life. That was Chris Wren's experience. Locked up in the grim place after being wrongfully accused of being part of a drug smuggling racket, he started reading the daily devotional out of sheer boredom.*

My ordeal came after I had had an enthusiastic response to my advertisement in a yachting magazine offering my services as a qualified skipper in September 1984. I flew with my girlfriend to Greece to charter a boat for businessmen and pleasure-seekers wanting to cruise the Mediterranean. The boat, a cutter called *Too Extravagant*, was only suitable for such a short trip.

As we headed southwards, two Lebanese boarded the vessel. Eventually the man who had hired me ordered us – my girlfriend, an English crewman and myself – to sail off the Cyprus coast. I was drugged and unconscious for two days. When I came round I found that they had taken the yacht to the coast near Jbail. It lay at anchor there for ten days. We were held at gunpoint, drugged, threatened and abused. Then the horrible truth dawned on me: the group weren't holidaymakers but drug smugglers! One of the Lebanese told us he was an assassin and would not hesitate to kill us if we did not co-operate. They had an armoury of guns, so we were helpless.

We left the area with over two tons of drugs with a street value of £6 million on board. When we approached Lisbon the engine broke down. As we wallowed there on 26 October 1984, armed Portuguese sailors boarded and all of us were arrested. Unknown to me at the time, this was part of the international anti-drugs operation called Tonic and our movements had been kept under surveillance by satellite.

I spent five months in jail. I wasn't badly treated, but conditions in that cell were grim – and I railed at the injustice of it all. Boredom was a big problem and for no particular reason other than that, I started reading a book handed to me called *Run Baby Run*, by Nicky Cruz, the New York drug-addicted gang leader converted to Christ through David Wilkerson's ministry. It was to pass the time – nothing else – that I also began reading a copy of *Every Day with Jesus* that someone who had heard of my plight had sent me. It was the November/December 1984 issue on the theme of *Strong at the Broken Places*, based on Hebrews 11:34 – '… whose weakness was turned to strength …'. I was struck by Selwyn Hughes' question of November 1: 'Have you been broken by life to such an extent that you feel an overwhelming sense of weakness?'

The booklet went on to state that when failure strikes we should 'face it in the knowledge that with God something can be made out of it'. Selwyn wrote about life breaking us with 'unmerited suffering and affliction' and exhorted readers to 'accept suffering as a gift from God'. Further on it explained God's remedy for each situation: the Lord Jesus Christ and His saving death on the cross.

I can't remember what part of the notes I was reading, but as I was absorbing the words one day I felt the Holy Spirit come upon me and all my anger and bitterness at the unjust treatment meted out to me leave me completely. I felt calm and invincible. God had reached out to me in a remarkable way. Now it didn't matter that I was in jail for something I had not done – I had become a Christian.

Eventually I was released after a huge campaign, with my father at the forefront, which included international media publicity and diplomatic pressure. I arrived back in England in August 1985 and eventually got involved with Morning Star Trust, a Christian charity in Chatham dockyard, Kent, that owned two sail training vessels. The main one is a 62-foot gaff ketch that can be booked by groups or individuals. I worked for the Trust as an unpaid volunteer from 1996 until 1999, while continuing to gain income from small property investments to pay off debts.

I left Morning Star in response to a request through RedR (Register of Engineers for Disaster Relief) from the OSCE, part of the UN, to work in Kosovo to help rebuild the country after the war. I helped in all matters technical, including the Pristina district central heating system, supply and installation of generators across the country and advising on building management matters. Although I was asked to continue at the end of my contract, I had already booked on a course to update my yachtmaster qualification and began to study for Yachtmaster Class IV (yachts up to 3,000 tons).

Despite gaining many qualifications and much experience in the marine field, I had surprisingly no success over many years in obtaining a permanent paid job afloat. So perhaps it was a part of God's plan that the only open door was an offer in May 2002 to skipper a Christian organisation's 95-foot gaff schooner in Greece. I made a commitment to again work as an unpaid volunteer – but this time permanently.

The vessel, *Genevieve Challenge*, was built by Tony Turner in Zimbabwe with the intention of using her for Christian purposes along the east coast of Africa. But after completing her he felt called to give her away and she is now run by the Release Foundation, supported by Kings Community Church, Bedworth, near Coventry. She can be booked by individuals or groups of up to 13 who join the permanent crew of skipper, cook and one or two deckhands. There is also a spiritual leader who may be appointed by the group or by the yacht owners.

In 2002 we sailed among the beautiful Sporades islands and Halkidiki in northern Greece. Most of the guests were Christians, including a number of missionaries on retreat. There were groups of teenagers who wanted to spread the gospel in schools through drama and songs, while one regular group leader brings together individual missionaries from all over the world for these trips, especially from Eastern Europe. The feedback I have received from the end of each *Genevieve Challenge* trip is resounding success every time. Many have found new direction to their lives by taking part.

I may not be a missionary in the traditionally accepted sense, but this is what God has called me to do. And for this I thank Him for allowing me to spend time in a Portuguese prison and using Selwyn Hughes' writing in *Every Day with Jesus* to change my life and turn it in the right direction.

FREED TO BE WHO I AM

Joanna Thompson

The founder of a pregnancy crisis centre in Basingstoke that became a catalyst for a UK and international network, Joanna Thompson came to Waverley Abbey House in 1991 to take part in the one-year Institute in Christian Counselling course. It was a turning point in her Christian walk and a new beginning. Just after completing the course the pregnancy crisis centres became part of CARE and Joanna became National Co-ordinator. She is currently Manager of CARE Centres Network and part of the CARE leadership team. Her husband, Philip, a businessman, is a member of the network's support team, while daughter-in-law Becky, married to their policeman son, Mark, helps out in the Basingstoke office. Daughter Charlotte was married in May 2003.

One of my favourite phrases is 'becoming the best expression of who I am in Christ'. When I began the one-year Institute in Christian Counselling course I had very little understanding of who I am in Christ. Although often appearing confident, in reality I was very insecure. I knew that God loved me, but I wanted approval and affirmation from others as well. It's quite natural to want others to like and appreciate you, but the problem was that I felt I would fall apart if I didn't get this affirmation. I believed that I needed to portray myself as mature, wise and spiritual to gain approval. Laughable really – especially to those who knew me well! I fitted so well into the CWR model of living under a self-made cloud of shame while trying to behave perfectly when others were looking so that I could avoid rejection. This only resulted in more shame when I tripped up.

I would, for example, go to a local house group meeting and be talkative, have no difficulty in sharing my thoughts and praying aloud. But back home I would think about what I had said at the meeting and if it wasn't perfect (which, of course, it never was) I would take the stick of self-contempt and berate myself for being too verbal, too loud, too foolish … Why couldn't I be like my quiet friend who appeared so wise, pondering things in her heart? Little did I know that she was wishing she could share like me! My way of coping was to resolve that I would say nothing; but I never managed it, which only added more fuel to the fires of self-contempt.

Through the CWR counselling course, and in particular the help I received from Jenny Trust, our senior tutor, I came to realise that this need for approval was, in essence, spiritual adultery. I knew God loved and accepted me as I was, but I was living as if this was not enough. To feel secure and at peace I needed to be noticed and accepted by others as well. Some of this may have come from being sent to boarding school at the age of five.

It has been life-changing to not only experience God's love and acceptance but in making the choice that His love is enough. This truth has been so liberating. It is also something I have to come back to constantly, as I can easily slip into trying to be what others expect me to be instead of just being myself and run the risk of being misunderstood. I've also come to see that others do not judge me as harshly as I judge myself. My friends and colleagues seem to enjoy me far more for just being me instead of trying to be this perfect person that is really quite unattractive! They are far more generous and gracious than I had given them credit for.

By the end of the course I really knew that God accepted me with all my weaknesses and faults, and that His grace, anointing and presence with me was all that counted. I realised that I could not earn this by trying to be perfect, but just needed to relax and enjoy it! The ICC course was a turning point in my Christian walk as well as a new beginning.

Long before I began that walk with Him, God had been at work in my life through the prayers of a Christian godmother who I had only met a few times. After I became a Christian I found out that I was the last of her six godchildren to be converted. She had prayed for us every day. She died just a few months after I had received Jesus as my Saviour and I shall always be grateful for her faithful intercession.

Some people come to Jesus because they recognise a real need in their lives. But it wasn't like that for me. It was only as I look back now that I see how needy I was. Sent to boarding school as a little girl and sexually abused as a child contributed to feelings of inadequacy and terror of being left out or rejected. People thought I was very secure but my true feelings were buried very deeply by the time I reached adulthood. I told myself that everything was great. My husband and I had a lovely home, good jobs and an exciting social life. Then a school friend came to stay. I knew she had 'religion' and didn't want that to interfere with my life, but I was curious. Although she irritated me with her certainties about life and death and I gave her a hard time, I couldn't stop thinking about what she had said. The Holy Spirit was busy with my thoughts.

A few weeks after she had left I was convinced that God was real and Jesus was alive. Nothing else made sense. But how could I respond? I tried bargaining with God, saying I would become a Christian on my deathbed – but I didn't know when that would be! What if I was run over by a bus? I thought becoming a Christian would mean giving everything up. It felt like stepping into a dark place. It was totally opposite.

I knelt in my bedroom and asked Jesus to forgive me for all my sins and, realising that He had given His life for me, I said I wanted to give my life to Him. No one had told me about the peace and joy that salvation brings. When I woke up the next morning I experienced God's presence in a wonderful way. Within three weeks I was baptised and filled with the Holy Spirit. God had begun the process of setting me free to be me.

In 1971 the house church movement was young. My friend with 'religion' went to one such fellowship and I travelled 60 miles each week to go with her. For the past 20 years I have been a member of Basingstoke Community Church, which came into being through the growth of that movement. One of the things I really enjoy about my work with CARE, however, is speaking in churches of many different denominations, including the Anglican Church, where I was confirmed many years ago. I've come to love and appreciate the many different ways Christians worship God and I'm grateful for the truths I heard in church as a child, even though it took years for understanding to dawn.

It was at Basingstoke Community Church, in a back room, that the first pregnancy counselling centre started. In the early 1980s abortion was high on the political agenda and to a small group of us it seemed that the woman with an unwanted pregnancy would be lost in the midst of the debate. We wanted to provide a safe place for her where she could look at her options and come to her own informed decision. We longed for her to choose life for her child and herself, but we weren't going to pressurise her. Rather, we would pray and trust God to work in her heart as we lovingly reached out to her. With the support of Christians from other churches in Basingstoke we opened the centre in 1984, advertising free pregnancy tests and support.

After a slow start women kept coming. We realised that God wanted us to help women who had had abortions as well. Then we were asked to go into local schools and talk about our work. Who would have thought that we would be standing in a classroom of 15-year-olds talking about sex! I think if we had known what God had in store for us we would have run a mile. But He has equipped us as we have stepped out trusting Him.

Other churches saw what we were doing and wanted to open centres. Soon there were centres across the south of England. We formed a networking body called Christians Caring for Life so that we could share ideas and encourage each other. By the time the number of centres had reached 40 we needed more help and CARE invited us to become part of their organisation. Their mission statement of declaring Christian truth and demonstrating Christ's compassion fitted so well with our work. In 1992, just after I had completed the Institute of Christian

Counselling course at Waverley, we became the CARE Centres Network (initially called CARE for Life) and I was appointed National Co-ordinator.

The Network has grown to 150 centres in the UK and many centres in other countries relate to us. We have a freephone national helpline which in 2002 received nearly 4,000 calls. There are thousands of children alive today because their mothers visited a centre. There are also many, many women who have experienced God's forgiveness for having an abortion and been able to grieve the loss of their child. Our focus now is moving to adoption, helping women who aren't in a position to parent to see this as a positive alternative to abortion. We want to come alongside birth mothers, supporting them while they seek to place their child in a loving family and discover God's plans for their life as well.

When I began the CWR course I had been a volunteer at the Basingstoke centre for six years. I could not possibly have imagined then all I would be doing now. So much of my life has been a preparation for it and my time at Waverley was an important part of it. My current role as Manager of the Network involves networking the pregnancy centres throughout the UK and helping Christians in other countries set up centres. Much of this work is based on relationships. I really enjoy encouraging others whom God has called to this work to be themselves. If they try to be something they think they should be then their work will be ineffective. God can only fill with His Spirit what is real.

With so many women under the illusion that they have to abort an unplanned pregnancy, the primary work of the centres involves helping them to look at the options and so come to realise that they do have a choice they can make with integrity. To be able to do this they need our unconditional acceptance. You cannot give what you have not received, so we need first to know and experience God's love, mercy and unreserved acceptance. Then we have something real to offer. So often this opens up the way to speak of the greater love of God. This ethos permeates all we do in the CARE Centres Network. In a word, it is grace.

In his book *What's So Amazing About Grace*, Philip Yancey says there is nothing we can do to make God love us more and nothing we can do to make Him love us less. I know that if God took His mercy from me I would make as many foolish decisions as many of the young people we seek to help are making. I am no different to them except that I have tripped over God's love and mercy – and I long for them experience this, too. Before I went on the CWR course I knew this in my mind, but living under the cloud of shame stopped me from living in the good of it.

Our support for women who have had abortions is based on grace. God longs for them to experience His compassion. So many of them are living in shame. What a privilege to share with women in Eastern Europe, many of whom have had between 10 and 20 abortions, that there is nothing they can do that could make God love them less. So many there believe abortion is the unforgivable sin. The tragedy is that a woman who has had an abortion can never hold that baby in her arms and has to live with that reality. She can, however, experience God's love, forgiveness and acceptance – just as I discovered for myself during the counselling course at Waverley.

FROM A SHACK
TO A CONTINENT

Gladys Mwiti

CWR is a catalyst for Christian counselling in many countries around the world. In 1989 Gladys Mwiti came to Waverley Abbey House from Kenya to take part in the first three-week Institute in Christian Counselling course. During it Oasis was born. Today it has grown from a shack in Gladys and husband Gershon's backyard, with a table and chair borrowed from their house, into a pan-African grassroots counselling and leadership organisation with a vision for the healing and reconstruction of Africa through its programmes.

I came into contact with CWR around 1986 through using *Every Day with Jesus*. I had previously used many remarkable devotionals, but as soon as I began using *EDWJ* I felt a spiritual connection that linked my faith with my daily experiences: thoughts, wishes, feelings, actions, relationships ... It was as if God and Selwyn Hughes began each of my days with a counselling session, the two talking with me about issues pertinent to current experiences and struggles. I started hungering for more of what I was reading and meditating on.

Through my mother's radiant influence I had become a Christian at seven years old. She was a product of the East African revival in the late 1930s and early 40s. I was among 4,000 others at a four-day open air convention when the preacher, after presenting God's love through John 3:16, asked: 'Since God loved you so much to give His only Son for your redemption, how much do you love Him in return?' I joined many others to receive Christ into my heart, with tears and a prayer, 'Lord, help me to love you just a little bit as you love me.' (I knew my love for Him could never equal His love for me). So began a journey of love, trust, faith and obedience.

Serving Him gradually became as natural as my daily breath. The starting point was on the next day after my conversion which was a Sunday. The church elders announced that I had become a Christian and I was asked to say what the Lord had done for me. I was lifted on to the rickety old table that served as an altar so that everyone could see this little girl. There I shared my first testimony. From then onwards I served the Lord through school, college, at church and in the community. Discipled through the East African revival at home, the Methodist Church in Kenya, Kenya Christian Students Fellowship and many other evangelistic groups, it was made very clear to me that serving the Lord is never an option for the believer.

For many years I preached, taught, counselled as a lay person, and discipled many people. However, as I worked with young people and their parents in schools, church and community, I noticed a yawning *values vacuum*. Tribal training in social relationships and ethics were replaced with Western education devoid of training within a Christian faith that did not translate pulpit messages into practical application. For example, while money and time was spent training people to become doctors and teachers, no similar training was offered to couples planning to get married or already in wedlock. No one seemed to prepare young people for adulthood, to equip them on values or etiquette.

In essence, Africa continued, and continues, to a large extent, to hang between the old and the new, with cultural ways unexploited and discarded as primitive but nothing replacing the lost richness of a culture that held people together and made the young accountable to their elders. Swayed hither and thither through immersion in 'Western' lifestyles, many young people were getting involved in premarital sex, teenage pregnancy, drugs, rebellion against parents and authority … I felt more and more the pull to respond to this brokenness and eventually, after teaching at high school for 13 years and married with four children, I started on the road to a ministry of counselling. This meant studying psychology at a secular university because that was as close as I could get to the subject in Kenya. I gained a BA in psychology in 1986, followed by an MA in counselling psychology three years later.

Throughout this training a hunger was growing for a way to integrate my faith and practice. How could I make Christ's presence and healing a central part of my work as a psychologist?

Then glory! Early in 1989 I saw an advert in *Every Day with Jesus* for the first Christian Counselling Institute to be held at Waverley Abbey House, led by Selwyn. The advert called especially for psychologists and other mental health professionals who would like to learn how to integrate their faith and practice. CWR and Tearfund paid my course fees, while the National Council of Churches in Kenya paid my air fare to the UK. During the course God spoke to me about the work He had been preparing me for. Oasis was born at Waverley Abbey House.

When I shared with Selwyn the vision God had given me to begin a faith counselling ministry in Kenya, he did not for a moment doubt that the voice came from God. In the quietness of that August afternoon at Waverley he said, 'Let us pray for our little counselling centre in Kenya.' Selwyn's greatest gift to me was to call things that *were not as though they were.* I knelt on the carpet and he laid hands on me, commissioning me in the Lord's service, and praying that I would faithfully follow His leading.

When I got home and shared with my husband, Gershon, and the children what the Lord had told me, we named this new baby Oasis. Selwyn has continued to pray and encourage us, visiting us several times in Kenya. He is a member of our International Board of Reference. Other staff, especially Jeannette Barwick, have also remained close to us.

When Oasis was born we based our lay counsellors' training on CWR's three-week model and used many of the Waverley materials, including Selwyn's understanding of humanity's need and God's provision for wholeness.

Oasis is a grassroots focused organisation. We work with leaders, but more so with ordinary individuals in communities across Africa. From the outset our focus has been on prevention and mental/relational health, rather than waiting for people to break down and marriages to get into trouble before they come looking for us to help them. This has led to a focus on empowering individuals and churches for change and transformation.

The ministry has three types of programmes: professional counselling at the centre; counsellor training seminars, development of training materials, and programme evaluation for supporting organisations; research and needs assessment. Oasis training focuses especially on the Church, Christian organisations and schools, with seminars for workers with children at risk, youth counsellors, women development programme coordinators, HIV and AIDS counsellors, trauma counsellors and leaders.

Oasis has trained over 500 people through these programmes who are working in 16 African nations. In addition there are 850 lay counsellors in Rwanda, the fruit of Oasis's trauma counsellor training after the 1994 genocide. In 2002, with a major focus on HIV and AIDS, we trained 2,253 counsellors, leaders, community care-givers and traditional birth attendants in Kenya, Cameroon and Rwanda. We have strong links with our graduates in the various African countries and we seek to help them strengthen and expand their ministries.

At present Gershon and I are studying at Fuller Seminary in America – myself at the Graduate School of Psychology and Gershon at the School of World Mission. I am aiming to obtain a PhD in clinical psychology and an MA in theology because I feel it will give me tools that could help me communicate in a more credible way to a complex Africa. I also view these studies as opening new doors, especially into secular circles, where I could impact things for Christ. This higher education would make Oasis a more efficient and listened-to organisation. This is a demand in the changing Africa. Gershon is working on a doctorate of Missiology in Christian Leadership. We hope to graduate together in June 2004. I am looking forward to completing my studies and going back to serve in Oasis Africa.

I view my training in psychology as a scalpel. Christ is the Healer of my people. I have asked Him for the healing of the wounds of Africa. I want to continue to be in the hand of the Healer, the hand that wields the scalpel, bringing healing and restoration.

SEEING DEATH IN THE RIGHT PERSPECTIVE

Jerry Bushell

In November 1997 Jerry Bushell and his wife, Suzanne, became members of 'a most horrible club' when their teenage daughter, Kate, was murdered in Exeter where they live. Soon afterwards they realised that God was also in this club. Six months after the tragedy, in the midst of their struggles adjusting to life without Kate, Jerry was uplifted through reading an issue of Every Day with Jesus *dealing with Life's Troublesome Emotions. One of the studies mentioned Kate's murder.*

———————————

I became a Christian in 1972 through an evangelical Anglican church youth club. The seeds of faith had been sown throughout my childhood in Sunday school, CSSM missions and other things, although it was probably my Christian mother's input and prayer that influenced me most. My father didn't become a Christian until after he and my mother divorced in 1978. One evening at a church youth club the curate gave an epilogue suggesting that if ever we needed a friend we could ask Jesus. Not long afterwards I left home to start work in a Midlands town where I knew nobody, so I asked Jesus to be my Friend.

Jesus became my best Friend and also introduced me to a lot of His friends about my own age – better and closer friends than I had had before.

In 1973 I went to Nottingham to train as a teacher and it was while I was at college that I experienced the baptism of the Holy Spirit. I also met Suzanne and we were married in a Baptist church in Nottingham. Both our children, Tim (now 21) and Kate, were born while we lived in the city. In 1988 I concertinaed my spine in a swimming accident, which disabled me for four months. In pain and desperation I drove to a healing service at our church and lay across a pew. The service was very calm and low key – and God healed me!

Moving to Devon, I worked until a stress breakdown in 1995 and illness from consequent depression led to early retirement. I had two wonderful years at home spending time with my family until 15 November 1997, when Kate took the dog belonging to a couple of friends out for a walk and she never came back.

The following May I was really moved to read the mention of Kate's murder in *Every Day with Jesus*. I wrote to Selwyn Hughes at the time to tell him that I knew it would stir the hearts of many, not least those many Christians who knew Kate and her love for Jesus. It seemed so appropriate that Selwyn had written this in a study on Life's Troublesome Emotions.

We have had to do a lot of adjusting as a family, often reappraising our view of God and of one another. We received help, especially from Christians prepared to give fully of their unconditional love. My church did everything possible to help and support us and I will always remember with gratitude the way they held us through a time when we couldn't have coped without them. But their support alone wasn't enough. I needed to know someone who could give hope despite having similar experiences. God had already provided. I had friends in a church in Bosnia who understood.

I can't underestimate the grace of God in providing for my need in another way before I knew of it. I was 15 months into being a trained as a counsellor when Kate was murdered. This provided me with a reliable group of people devoid of religious cliché who both helped me and at the same time gained in their understanding of grief.

Where has God been in all this? The morning after Kate's murder I remember saying to Suzanne that we were members of a most horrible exclusive club, parents of murdered children. It was a few days later that we realised that God is also in this club. He had been there before us.

That Christmas I asked God how we were going to cope with a lifetime of Kate not being there. The answer didn't come for a few days, then it was as though I had a conversation with Kate: 'How are you going to spend Christmas in heaven? It must be quite an enormous celebration there.' 'We don't. You see, for us Christmas is a time of loss …'.

I began to see the enormity of the gift. I almost felt it offensive to God that we do so much to celebrate the time when He gave up His Son eventually to die, but God wants us to fully appreciate the wonderful gift He has given. Again, I knew that God had been there before us.

As we were clearing out Kate's bedroom, it was as if I had another 'conversation' with her. I could almost hear her crying, so I asked: 'Why are you crying? Heaven isn't meant to be a place of tears.' 'No, but you are in a place of pain and suffering and I'm crying because of your pain …'.

The pain goes on, but it has changed my perspective of

heaven and dying. Now I know that death is an event to be looked forward to with joy and anticipation, not with fear, and that at the right time it will be Jesus who comes to take each of us home to be with Him for ever. In times of grief I haven't wanted to wait, but I know that the choice of time is God's and not mine – just as it was for Kate.

This looking forward to death as a positive event has grown a little more since the death of my father in 2000 and my mother early in 2001. Having lived into his eighties, Dad came to the conclusion that if he couldn't be well enough to attend my youngest brother's wedding he'd rather not be around. It seems God answered his desire. After a road accident medical treatment seemed no longer to be effective. His funeral was in June and the wedding took place the following month.

My mother never really got over the loss of Kate, which happened shortly after the deaths of her older sister and brother. She began to suffer senile dementia, then the part of the brain causing the dementia closed down and for a couple of months she was restored. But slowly and with no apparent pain, her body and brain functions all quietly and peacefully closed down until there was nothing but a small, frail corpse, Mum had already left to be for ever with Jesus.

Now I know there is rightness about death in the way God orders it.

Every Day with Jesus has continued to be an amazing help. I began using it in the early 1970s and there have been so many instances when the study passage and meditation were straight from God.

After Kate's death, I took time out before I resumed training in counselling. I qualified in 2001, two years later than planned, and have been part of Crossline in Exeter since then. There are a number of Crossline ministries in Britain. They began about 25 years ago as telephone helplines and all now provide Christian counselling. Some also have other ministries: in Exeter Crossline also provides food and clothing for homeless people.

I have also taken specialist training in traumatic incident reduction. Normal counselling training would tell you not to try to handle things too close to your own experience and never to assume your experience means you can prescribe for or resolve anyone else's pain. But God seems willing to use our wounds to deepen our understanding. At the same time, God heals. However much I may have applied specialist training or interventions, I can never predict how a counselling situation will develop, or cease to wonder at the healing God brings.

Not long before the swimming accident, in seeking God's guidance for my life, I was encouraged to pray to know not just God's will, but His heart. I think I've come to know a little of that heart since then.

HEARING
MIRACULOUSLY RESTORED

Gloria Hart

Gloria Hart has been a CWR Partner since Waverley Abbey House opened in 1987. God has called her to be an intercessor there. Over the years she has been involved with the women's ministry and it was on one such weekend at Waverley that she experienced God's miraculous power of healing her deteriorating hearing.

———————————

The road to faith in Christ began for me when my Christian mother sent me to a Church of England Sunday school. I was confirmed at 14, feeling the Christian life was the best way of living. Then I had the choice of Sunday school teaching or the choir. I couldn't sing so I did Sunday school until I married at 21 and left home. At 23 I read a book, *The Robe*, by Lloyd C Douglas and the whole thing changed into reality and I experienced the living Christ with me. This went on for quite a few years before we came to settle in Frimley, Surrey, with our son, Paul, who was at primary school. There was a curate at our local church there who had something different about him. I had migraines that were hitting me twice a week. Just before he was due to leave the parish this curate held a healing service and the shy little mouse that was me went forward. Me talk to the curate? Joke! But I just had to – I was suffering from another migraine. It was through his gentle questions that I subsequently asked Jesus into my life and was baptised in His Spirit.

I joined a ladies house group and was introduced to *Every Day with Jesus*. Further contact with CWR came through attending

Caring seminars in London and my first counselling course in Guildford. My husband, David, and I got to know about the purchase of Waverley Abbey House and over many months looked at the blue tarpaulin over the roof of the building. After Lord Tonypandy had officially opened Waverley we went to a prayer meeting that involved walking through the buildings and over the grounds and we decided to become Partners.

It was at a marquee meeting that God called me to be an intercessor at Waverley. He spoke clearly and directly, which is unusual for me. He said: 'Your ministry is intercession and it's here.' So I have been involved with those intercessory prayer mornings from the start. They're vital – I can't see any hope for this country and for the world apart from revival.

The Women's Ministry is very special. At these weekends no one cares about what denomination we belong to, whether we're wives, parents, single, what career we may have – we're all sisters in Christ. We throw off the hats we wear and share some very deep things. We're made to feel loved, important and special to God.

My life and relationships have been transformed and enriched through many different experiences at Waverley and especially through being involved in the women's events. *Every Day with Jesus*, the *Cover to Cover* Bible study series and many CWR courses, including a three-week counselling course David and I attended some years ago, have also helped me grow and mature as a Christian.

What stands out most, however, is my experience of being prayed for during the Handfuls on Purpose women's weekend in June 2002. It is still living in my memory and I expect, quite honestly, that it always will. During the Saturday evening fellowship we were in the lounge praying for one another. Right at the last minute I requested prayer for difficulties relating to a hearing loss, a problem that had steadily grown worse over some 20 years. Even with two hearing aids it was seriously limiting participation in many discussions.

The sisters brought my need to the Throne of Grace. Then, quite unexpectedly, one of the team asked the Lord to heal my ears. Amazingly, He did there and then! It was such a shock – it really was. I also found it so thrilling, once I had got over the shock – which took me a couple of days.

This divine touch has transformed my everyday life in many remarkable ways. The healing is so real that I cannot get to sleep at night if the tap is dripping in the next room. And my husband is delighted that he can now speak to me without either having to shout or stand in front of me. He is also very aware that he can no longer get away with the quiet side comments he has been making on occasions for the past 15 years! I am so full of thanks and praise to my loving heavenly Father and delight in sharing my testimony to give honour to His name. It's all of Him and none of me because I didn't have any faith to be healed. It proves that Jesus is not only alive, which I knew, but He's *around*!

COUNSELLING COURSE
MY BIGGEST HELP

Jennifer Rees Larcombe

Many Christians are living testimonies to the fact that God brings good out of terrible, seemingly impossible situations. Jennifer Rees Larcombe is one of them. Struck down by an illness that confined her to a wheelchair for eight years, she has become a prolific author, counsellor and speaker. Today she leads a ministry to hurting women appropriately called Beauty from Ashes. She spends a lot of time with women whose marriages are in trouble or, like hers, have broken up. CWR's ministry, especially Bible reading notes and counsellor training, has had a significant impact on her Christian walk.

I became a Christian when I was a child, when my mother explained how we can open the door of our hearts and let Jesus in. I was sitting in a car in Germaine Street, London, when I opened my heart to Him. My parents ran Hildenborough Hall, the well-known Christian conference centre. They both wrote Christian books and spoke about Christ all around the world. They were such good examples of the Lord's love that it was as easy to catch their faith as it was to catch measles in those days!

I ended up in a wheelchair after being struck by a brain virus, similar to meningitis. It damaged my brain and central nervous system. Every time I got any kind of infection it flared up again and left me even more disabled. Yet it was while I was stricken with this illness that I wrote a bestseller called *Beyond Healing* and this made me widely known in the Christian world both at home and abroad. The book was about *not* being healed and how we can hold on to our faith even when God does not answer our prayers.

Then I was suddenly healed through the prayers of a new Christian – which caused a bit of a sensation! By that time I had also written a number of other books, so people were very interested in what had happened to me. My healing led to all kinds of invitations to speak and a lot of requests for books, TV interviews, videos … I have written 28 books now. I began as a children's writer and then wrote about the problem of suffering and unanswered prayer. I wrote about healing after being healed, but I have also gone on to write Christian novels and fantasy books.

I began reading the Bible with daily notes at the age of 12. My first contact with CWR's ministries came through using *Every Day with Jesus*. The *Cover to Cover* series blessed me profoundly. Until then I had skipped about – a book from the Old Testament, a few Psalms, then a Gospel and a bite of Revelation. To tackle the whole Bible chronologically in one year was wonderful! I suddenly realised where all those minor prophets actually fitted and why David wrote his Psalms the way he did. I am the kind of person who needs a definite plan of Bible readings; otherwise I binge on the Psalms and Gospels and leave the tougher books!

Recently CWR invited me to contribute to the new devotional, *Inspiring Women Every Day*. I wrote about David, whom I have always loved and often spoken about. Writing this series of daily thoughts gave me a totally new insight into him as a man. I have so often concentrated on his relationship with

God, which we can see so clearly in the Psalms, but I had never studied his other relationships. I was amazed how badly he did with some of them! He was a terrible father! And several other relationships were not a good idea. This gives me a lot of comfort; he was so human and so am I.

The other way CWR has helped me is through counsellor training courses. After being healed I began to work more and more with people who were grappling with losses of all kinds and felt that a counselling course would really help me to understand them. So I did a three-week residential course at Waverley Abbey House and then the one-year Institute in Christian Counselling course there. CWR has helped me enormously in my speaking and writing and I would say that the counselling training was the most helpful thing in all my 38 years of full-time ministry!

It was while doing a Myers-Briggs course at Waverley that I discovered I am a 'feelings' person – led by my heart rather than being a 'thinking' person led by the head. I guess a lot of women are like that, perhaps more so than men.

I speak at ladies' events at Waverley. My first talk, about eight years ago, was on forgiveness. I once spoke there on angels. I dressed up as an imaginary one and tried to tell the story of God's secret plan for the human race through angel eyes. I did another talk during Advent, when I interviewed (in imagination) all the various people connected with the Christmas story and asked them what they would like to say to us 2000 years on. Another subject was on relationships and how we can improve them.

Beauty from Ashes, which is based at Hildenborough, near Tonbridge in Kent, is a healing centre. Our aim is to support those adjusting to loss and trauma. This might be the loss of a marriage, health, the death of someone close or being made redundant. We hold Quiet Days regularly. People can come and just 'be' or they can book a slot with me or one of my team for prayer and a chance to talk. We also offer private appointments for people to come when they wish. I work with a doctor and a team of trained counsellors and others skilled in prayer ministry. We also run five-day breaks for people who are coming to terms with loss. We take them away to a lovely place where they can relax and rest, and have teaching on the effects of loss – physical, mental, emotional and spiritual. They can also book daily appointments with one of the team.

My vision for the future is to go on supporting and loving people for as long as I can. As I pursue this vision I thank God for the help, insights and inspiration He has given me through CWR's ministries.

CLARIFYING
AN INDIAN VISION

Samson Gandhi

Three weeks attending an Institute in Christian Counselling course in 1996 deeply ministered to Samson Gandhi and confirmed his calling. Back home in India he had a struggle with leaving the 'land of milk and honey' – his secure position with Haggai Institute – before taking the necessary step of faith to start Person to Person based on the skills he had learned at Waverley. Samson is Executive Director of PtP, which has grown into a counselling ministry impacting the Church in India and beyond.

I come from a Christian middle class family. Dad was a police inspector and Mum a teacher before they retired. I gave my life to Christ when I was 19 at a Youth for Christ meeting. My wife, Christine, and I have three children and we are actively involved in St John the Baptist Anglican Church in Hyderabad, south central India. From my early Bible study days I was convinced that God had a plan for our lives. I set out to know it.

Talking to several mature Christians, I learned that I could discover the talents God had given me. But before I heard of *counselling*, people were telling me that my listening to them and giving a few bits of advice had helped them a lot. When I asked if there was a gifting like that I was told it was 'encouraging' (Romans 12:8). The Lord subsequently confirmed this through my experiences.

I wanted to go into 'full-time' ministry when I graduated from university, but my parents wanted me to study further before doing so. What my parents were unable to convey, one of my aunts did – although she was not a trained counsellor. I knew there were many like me who needed such people to listen to them and seek godly guidance. Although I went on to gain a MBA degree I did lay my desire to serve Him on His altar. After 11 years of waiting God confirmed His calling and fired me with a vision to start the kind of ministry I head now.

For a long time I searched for a Bible-centred Christian counsellor training course. Then in 1993 I chanced upon a copy of *Every Day with Jesus*, which mentioned such courses. Attending one of them immediately became a priority prayer request!

But nothing happened for three years. My praying became desperate and I was asking God, 'What is happening?' Then I distinctly heard Him say, 'Samson, do you really think that CWR will teach you more than I can?' It hit me like a bolt out of the blue. I clearly saw that CWR's training programme had become an idol in my life. So I said, 'Lord, here and now I drop it.' And off my prayer list it went. But within three months I was at Waverley for the three-week Introduction to Christian Counselling course. It was so clear that I was called by God to be there. He made it possible because the course fee was beyond my means – six months of my salary as a middle level business executive at that time. The other remarkable thing was the return air fare to the UK – said to be lower than going by road. It came in handy!

Those three weeks at Waverley in August 1996 redefined my personality, made me more like Christ and set the path for my ministry. It was like a confirmation and a commissioning.

I came to England to learn about counselling, but I came away counselled. That, perhaps, was the best that could have happened. I thought I had surrendered everything to God and told myself that my entire security was in Him. But through the counselling I received at Waverley I realised that although God *was* my security I was still looking for recognition through ministry. This was revealing, to say the least. It changed my whole perspective on Christian work. It caused me to see that unless God was everything to me my ministry was finished. In that sense the revelation was a redefining moment in my life.

The counselling model that was presented on that course was so simple yet so profound and so powerful that I knew what lay ahead. I knew how to go about what God was calling me into. The course helped me to fine-tune the vision He had given me.

But it was one thing being oriented, knowing that I must be about my heavenly Father's business, and another actually stepping out in faith. I returned to India to resume my work with Haggai Institute, an international Christian organisation which gives leadership training. I was doing well, handling finance and administration and being responsible for the work in the region. I was even seen as a future head of the organisation. To leave it was like departing from a land of 'milk and honey'. Maybe an even more appropriate metaphor was that I was like Peter – wanting to build a few booths on Mount Hermon when Jesus said there was work to be done in the valley. But the exposure and experience at CWR was so strong and the conviction from the Lord so sure that I decided to leave HI in 1997 and start Person to Person – Institute for Christian Counselling.

I had shared my vision for this ministry with many people. I was given much encouragement but quite a few said that the time had not yet come. The Lord strengthened me. Many leading Christians in Hyderabad joined hands with me and Person to Person was born. Since then it has been steadily growing and many lives have been changed. Our centre is in Secunderabad, just outside the city of Hyderabad, where Christians from all denominations come for counselling and counsellors are trained. Many who come to us feel rejected in society and find PtP a safe haven in which they are loved and accepted.

One of the most dramatic fruits of my ministry came after a woman who regularly passed the centre kept on noticing our PtP sign. Things were bitter between her and her 13-year-old daughter and degenerated into violence. One day the girl threw chilli powder into her eyes and threatened to kill her with a knife. On impulse, she phoned PtP and spoke to my wife, who told her to come to the centre right away. We counselled the two of them, had dinner together and the problem was resolved. The girl fell fast asleep at the centre – all stress gone. It was very touching, just to be available for them – to talk, listen and help. After all, that's what the Master did.

PtP's counselling is, of course, based entirely on biblical principles. Research findings in psychology are blended only to the extent they pass, as Dr Larry Crabb puts it, 'the Judgment bar of the Scriptures'. Marriage, pre-marital, family, grief, youth, careers, addictions and psychological disorder are some of the areas where counselling is provided at the centre. Some seek counselling by telephone, others through correspondence.

Our dream is to see every Christian who has been robbed of 'abundant life' regaining it (John 10:10) as they apply Scripture to everyday life and relationships. We see this happening as we train biblical counsellors for the Church, help to open and run counselling centres in churches throughout India that are a witness to the gospel, and organise seminars on practical and relevant issues so crucial to Christian growth.

Counselling in India is not as widely accepted as in the West. People still have their reservations, so many do not come for systematic counselling. Therefore we have adapted the CWR model to meet the needs of our sub-continent. The CWR model is fine when both counsellor and counsellee are aware of the process and are committed to staying with it until the problem is resolved. In India people want more advice and less exploration and seeking resolution with a counsellor. 'Tell us what to do and we will do it' is often the thinking.

Take, for example, a middle-aged father who came to us for counselling on how to improve communication with his daughter to overcome the growing distance between them. His troubled marriage was the real cause of the problem, but he was not willing to address it at the time. So our approach was to build up a relationship to develop in him enough trust and courage to address it, while at the same time I was helping him to develop communication with his daughter on a practical level. In the CWR model the counsellor would make a mental note of the communication problem and explore more on the marriage side, the crux of the issue.

CWR's counselling model is comprehensive and to offer it at

the training level requires time. We have adapted it to fit a shorter time scale.

We take our training programmes, ranging from three to seven days, to different parts of India. They are especially welcomed by Christian organisations that need trained counsellors for their ministries. Christian Mission Service, for example, provides care for over 7,000 orphan and semi-orphan children all over the country. We did counsellor training programmes for all their child care staff and now they have their own counselling department. Several schools and colleges have introduced counselling as a result of our work.

While mainly Indians attend our courses, we have also trained Danes, Australians, Americans, Malays and some Europeans. We did a course with Youth With A Mission and half the participants were foreigners.

Recently I helped to form an Association of Christian Counsellors, an accreditation body, to help give PtP the necessary recognition both in India and abroad. I am amazed at how God has put PtP in a strategic position to make this happen. We thought we would like to see an ACC in India in ten years, but He made it happen in less than five. We had our first All India Counsellors' Conference in January 2002 and now we have ACC in place, with myself as its secretary. Word of Life Trust took the initiative to make it possible and I am delighted that Selwyn Hughes is one of ACC's advisers. God is moving PtP more and more into a place where we will be seen as a counsellor training centre of excellence. Within the next five years we hope to see the centre recognised internationally and providing counsellor training in South Asian countries.

My business experience, Haggai training and theological studies were all part of God's preparation for my ministry. They perfectly complemented counsellor training at CWR. PtP was established after 15 years of prayer and it was in the 14th year that I came to Waverley. The Introduction to Christian Counselling course there has become a reference point to assess my interpersonal relationships and has helped me to understand biblical truths more effectively. Since then I have been unpacking and applying it to my own life and to others.

FOLLOWING JESUS EVERY DAY

Nia Jones

A Christian singer and songwriter, Nia Jones has spent the last 16 years travelling the world in her ministry. Wherever she is, Nia uses Every Day with Jesus *to help her study God's Word. After being especially challenged in one issue of* EDWJ *she was inspired to write a song,* I Will Follow. *Her call is to spread the gospel to a world in need through her God-given gifts. As co-founder of the Smiles Foundation and Honorary Vice-President of Operation Christmas Child UK, her mission work has taken her to many countries, including Armenia, Romania, Serbia, Kosovo, Macedonia, Honduras, Belize and Tanzania. She has released 16 albums in English and four in her native Welsh. She has hosted her own Gospel Show with BBC Radio Cymru and Radio Wales and often appears on Welsh television.*

I've known of CWR's work for many years and met many people who use *Every Day with Jesus* in their Bible studies. One of the main things *EDWJ* has done for me has been to challenge me to discipline myself to get into God's Word every day. Before I started using the notes I had not been doing this. Sometimes I let it go for about three days, even as long as three weeks on occasions. It was all too easy in a busy life to let my devotions slip. But the date next to each day's passage in *EDWJ* acts as a wake-up call!

There's a tendency to think that pastors and others who share their faith from the platform have really got it all together. They are seen as men and women who get up early, spend a couple of hours or so in prayer and then walk close to God for the rest of the day. It's certainly not like that for me! I've struggled, not with loving God or knowing His love, but with organising myself enough to spend time sitting at His feet like Mary did, rather than being busy doing things like Martha. *Every Day with Jesus* has helped me structure this better.

As I travel eight months of the year it's great, too, that I do my daily study knowing that my best friend back home is doing the same. So even though we're apart, we're doing it together, and that helps me to feel connected with home even when I'm many miles away.

EDWJ has been such a source of encouragement to me to continue on the path God has set for my life, especially in the last year or so. I was especially struck by Selwyn Hughes' words in the study of 15 April 2002: 'Jesus' command is a challenge not to settle for anything less than what the Father wants to give us and wants to do with our lives …' Through this I was inspired to write a song:

I WILL FOLLOW

I don't want to settle for good or for better
When I know that you want the very best for my life
As the winds of change blow through my very soul
I will let go of the reins and I'll follow on

   Follow to the ends of the earth
   Follow by staying right at home
   Follow when I'm tired and when it hurts

Follow when I'm walking on my own
I don't really know when or where He'll lead me
But this one thing I know
I will follow on

I can just about see the difference between
The good and the bad the wrong and the right
But better and best it's a far greater test
So this I'll leave to my Maker but I will follow on

(Nia Jones © Global Music 2002.
From the album *Small Things*)

I need to follow Him, even into danger zones if need be. For others, following Him means staying at home and being His witness there, which is equally important to travelling the world. A minister friend of mind, an international speaker, trainer of pastors and author, has been forced to spend more time at home through health problems. He told me jokingly that *I Will Follow* challenged him so much about serving Him 'right at home' that he skips that track when he plays the CD! For people who have followed the Lord to the ends of the earth to fulfil His calling it can be a real struggle to come to terms with the fact that God can still use us very much at home.

I became a Christian when I was ten, having been brought up in a Christian family in Wales. I knew I needed Christ to guide and direct my life. I was baptised as a teenager in the outdoor baptism pool at the rural Welsh evangelical church our family attended. There were about 15 young people in a congregation of 50–60 and we formed a strong bond. We started a band, which was primitive to say the least, especially as the drummer's 'instrument' was a dustbin! At 11 I was the youngest member of the band and it stretched me musically and spiritually.

We always prayed together before rehearsals and concerts. This was a marvellous time for me, being with young people whom I looked up to. We really cared for each other, praying not only for the songs we sang and the people who would hear them, but family life, schoolwork … .

I still see most of the group from time to time when I go home to Wales. All of us continue to walk with the Lord. Some are ministers, ministers' wives and missionaries. Much of what we do today stems from those younger days of growing in the faith together and seeing God at work in our lives.

Now I live in Leeds and when I'm there I attend the South Leeds Church of the Nazarene. I don't lead worship or take part up front, apart from the children's slot once a year, for these are times for me to be refreshed and take in the teaching. It's a small, loving church where everyone knows each other. There is an outreach programme among the homeless and drug abusers in the city and it's exciting to see God at work through this.

I've been in full-time ministry as a contemporary Christian artist since 1987, but since 1997 mission has had as much emphasis as my music. I'm committed to go wherever God opens doors. Through Operation Christmas Child, part of Samaritan's Purse International led by Franklin Graham, I have shared the love of Christ among many people in countries suffering from war, poverty and natural disaster. Profits from the

... and alone on deck

*Chris Wren (second from right) with the
Kisi-Kids schools outreach group ...*

*Joanna Thompson addressing a CARE
event at the Royal Albert Hall*

Gladys Mwiti

Jerry Bushell

Gloria Hart – hearing restored

Samson Gandhi

Jennifer Rees Larcombe

Helena Wilkinson

Nia Jones in Romania with Operation Christmas Child

Angelo Grazioli

Daphne Cox with The Friday Girls

Camilla Douglas

*Varujan (far left) and Emma Smallwood
at the YWAM base in Brazil*

Roselyn Abbott

*Olivia Kyambadde speaking
at a Police Day in Uganda*

*Nigel James
at Waverley Abbey House*

Lynn Penson

sale of my albums have sponsored my trips and many gifts from Christians around the world have provided essential aid to orphanages and schools, Bibles for churches, medical supplies and much more.

The Smiles Foundation, which I co-founded in 2000, is an extension of my ministry. Through this charity over 1,000 people, mostly children, are able to have a meal every day. Children in Honduras are encouraged to attend school through knowing that they will have a hot lunch there. In Armenia more than 60 people in Shahumyan water tank village, which I first visited in 1997 on an Operation Christmas Child shoebox gifts distribution trip, are now attending church through us starting a soup kitchen, providing a daily meal for residents, paying electricity costs and supplying heaters for the harsh winter months.

In 2001 we began supporting needy families in and around Oradea, Romania, with monthly food supplies. Soon we were helping families meet housing and living costs as many faced eviction or doing without running water, electricity and fuel for the winter. We were also faced with families being split up and children being taken into institutional care because their homes were unfit for them to be brought up in. The Smiles Foundation responded by launching a project, sponsored by individuals and churches, through which homes are renovated – often by volunteers on mission trips – and other dwellings bought back for evicted families to be reunited.

I spend six months of each year in the USA, singing in churches and as a missionary guest at conferences, camps and vacation Bible study events. Some people ask me if I am a musician or a missionary. I guess I'm a musicianary!

Life has certainly not been dull since I obeyed God's call to follow Him and use the talents He has given me. My travels have brought me lots of stories – some funny, some sad, but my favourites are the ones where God has shown His faithfulness to me. And I am so grateful for *Every Day with Jesus*, which helps to keep me spiritually disciplined and learning from Him through His Word.

VICTORY OVER ANOREXIA

Helena Wilkinson

As a teenager, Helena Wilkinson had a serious problem: anorexia. Then she met Jesus and handed Him not only her life, but also her anorexia. She subsequently wrote a book, Puppet on a String, *about her battle with the eating disorder and it became a bestseller. Coming to Waverley as an Institute in Christian Counselling student and then joining CWR's staff proved life-transforming. Today she is Director of Kainos Trust, a Christian charity she founded to help eating disorder sufferers and those who support them.*

I was 18 when I walked hesitantly into a Christian youth camp and immediately found myself surrounded by a sea of faces. As usual, my feelings of shame and unworthiness resulted in a strong sense of being on the outside, but something seemed less threatening about these people – they had a joy and a security I longed for and I kept asking myself what it was they had that I didn't? The answer was JESUS!

I had known about Jesus for as long as I could remember and had fond memories of a picture in my bedroom of the face of a young girl cupped in His large, tender hands with other children gathered around, gazing at Him in wonderment. As a child I saw Jesus as a kind, gentle man who helped those in trouble. As a teenager I talked to Him about my agonising loneliness and questions about life.

When I was 16 my desperate search for answers to my ongoing emptiness and pain opened the door to a more intimate relationship with Jesus. In an attempt to survive past traumas, I found myself seriously ill in hospital with anorexia. Confronted one night with crippling emotional agony and physical sensations of sinking, I cried out to God to either take away my life or do something to help me. A figure appeared at the end of my bed, which I now know to be an angel, and I knew something had changed. Soon after this a Christian lady on the ward had a prophetic message for me: that I would come through anorexia knowing Jesus, that my name would be in print, that I would be well known for having had anorexia and that I would go on to help others!

Two years later, when I turned up at that Christian youth camp still caught in the anorexic trap, I had more or less forgotten about the prophecy. But after a couple of days of hearing the gospel being explained in a way that made sense to me, I had the revelation that Jesus is more than just a good man – He is the Son of God who died and rose again, and paid the price for my sin so that I could be restored to God and know His unconditional love. I sensed I was at the biggest crossroads of my life. I also knew if I was to follow Jesus I must give Him not only my life, but also my anorexia. This felt like an almost impossible sacrifice, but in my heart I knew that the time had come for me to surrender everything to Him. As I did so, I felt the power of the Holy Spirit on me. In front of me hung the crucified Christ – an awesome experience.

The following months consisted of being captivated by God's Word. The Psalms in particular spoke to me and I was overwhelmed with the author's honesty of emotion and acknowledgement of the sovereignty of God despite his pain and anger. God took me through a process of unravelling the mystery of why I had been bound by anorexia, depression and self-loathing and I wrote down my findings with a sense of urgency. I had little confidence in my writing, having failed my English Language 'O' level GCE twice and was still a teenager, but I felt sure that God was leading me to send my story to a literary agent. He read my story and replied the same morning, saying that it was compelling reading and that I would write many more books! Within three weeks I had signed a contract with a publisher and the book went on to be a bestseller.

Little did I realise that the publication of *Puppet on a String* in 1984 would evoke the response it did: an increasing demand for help from desperate people and a fascination by the media, resulting in a plethora of newspaper, radio and TV interviews. Two years later at the age of 22, in an attempt to escape being consumed by sufferers and media alike, I fled to Zululand to work as a research assistant for a Christian psychiatrist, who assured me that in his 25 years of working amongst the rural people he had not once come across a case of anorexia. A few months later a 16-year-old Zulu girl with anorexia appeared in outpatients and I was asked to see her! Word soon got round and requests to see sufferers in other towns came in, along with 60 speaking engagements all over South Africa!

Once more I found myself hunted down by the media in a quest to explain the mysteries of eating disorders, and I returned to England in the knowledge that I could not escape God's call upon my life! Around this time I was reading *Every Day with Jesus* and in the centre of that issue there was a double-page spread about a new building CWR was purchasing – Waverley Abbey House. I knew very little about CWR, but as I looked at the artist's impression of the completed building God clearly said that I would be working there! I thought it most strange at the time, since I was employed as a nanny!

Not long after this I decided to train in counselling and considered the forthcoming course at the newly restored Waverley Abbey House. My application was accepted, and in January 1989 I became a student on the first Institute in Christian Counselling course. I devoured the teaching and devotional time like a baby bird, wide beaked and thrusting its head forward in eager anticipation of being fed. I began to make sense of the nature of God and man and the sufficiency of Scripture in addressing man's problems in the physical, emotional, volitional, rational and spiritual areas of functioning. My eyes were opened to the real problem in life – how hungry we all are for love and how, since God is love, we are in fact hungry for Him! I realised that, as a result of the Fall, man's attributes of security, self-worth and significance became needs. These unmet needs lead us to developing our own ways of coping that fail us and remove God from His rightful place in our lives. This was a challenge to me personally as well as for my attempts to help other people.

While I was still on the course Selwyn told me that CWR wanted to start a new journal for Christian counsellors and asked if I would become the editor. So in January 1990, only a couple of weeks after completing my training, I joined CWR's full-time staff. It all happened so quickly that to begin with I had something of an identity crisis as I walked into 'staff only' areas still feeling like a student!

Being involved with CWR radically changed my life. Besides teaching me so much about the underlying causes of people's problems and a biblical approach to helping people, I believe my time as a student for one year and as a member of staff in the editorial and counselling departments for four years was crucial in preparing me for leadership. Amongst other things, my confidence grew and I became acquainted with good biblical principles and high standards for running an organisation.

Towards the end of working at Waverley I was commissioned by a publisher to write a comprehensive book on eating disorders, *Beyond Chaotic Eating*. It marked the beginning of a new chapter in my life: the setting up of Kainos Trust, a Christian charity for eating disorder sufferers and those supporting them. The Trust is committed to helping people through counselling, teaching, prayer, residential courses, writing and creative arts.

The Trust has been functioning since 1995 and people are continually asking for help. The problem sometimes is sufficient people to help them! But God is opening up new avenues, enabling the work to grow and expand as we join forces with another Christian charity in Gloucestershire, Word for Life Trust. This shows me God's heart for community, fellowship and pooling of resources. We all need each other; we are, after all, only one part of the Body! As we work with each other, not only can we use the gifts we have, but be challenged to develop those gifts. I am pleased to still be asked by CWR to use my gifts of lecturing and writing, and I am grateful to have the opportunity to develop the latter in contributing to the *Inspiring Women Every Day* Bible study notes. A new venture for me: what next I wonder?

BUILT ON THE
RIGHT FOUNDATIONS

Angelo Grazioli

Training at Waverley Abbey House reshaped Dr Angelo Grazioli's approach to his work as a professional counsellor and has been a key factor in his growing international ministry. He is the founder and director of the Sex Education and Dysfunction Unit in South Africa and an ordained Church of England in South Africa minister and the denomination's Registrar. Governments and organisations use him as a consultant on social, moral and ethical matters and his work has been recognised by several international awards. He has regularly presented seminars at Waverley on the biblical perspective of sex and sexuality, as well as leading CWR seminars in Asia on that subject and on preparation for marriage. With a degree in medicine as well as theology, he has devoted two decades to marital and sexological counselling. He is currently heading up a busy medical and emergency evacuation centre in Azerbaijan, Central Asia, while ministering to the local and expatriate Christian community there. Italian-born, Angelo and his Dutch wife, Janneke, have two grown-up sons and live in Cape Town, South Africa.

I heard the gospel and was saved while I was a first year medical student. By the time I graduated as MB ChB (Bachelor of Medicine/Surgery) from the University of Cape Town in the late 1970s, I was involved in counselling seekers who responded to the altar call at the strongly evangelical Cape Town church where I became involved in ministry. This ministry made me acutely aware of the lack of Christian resources in counselling at the time

– especially sexual matters. The Lord then made it very clear that He was calling me to be a professional practitioner in this field and led me to study sexology in Chicago, USA. This was followed by a degree course at the University of Western Cape, from where I graduated with a BTh (Bachelor of Theology) Honours cum laude.

After coming to Waverley Abbey House for Christian Counsellor training and several other formative courses, I soon developed a warm and mutually respectful relationship with Selwyn Hughes and with that other internationally known expert in the Christian counselling field, Larry Crabb Jr. I applied Selwyn's and Larry's basic biblical principles to a variety of sexological issues, developing biblical models which I tested and refined through interaction with the faculties of British, Australian and South African theological colleges.

In my years of clinical counselling practice many opportunities have presented themselves to build and grow strong on the biblically sound foundations laid by CWR. Membership of the first State President's HIV-AIDS Advisory Board was the beginning of much work in aspects of this epidemic that has changed the face of Africa. God has used my seminars to inspire a number of people to devote themselves to full-time ministry in this area of need. Some launched care centres that have reached thousands.

My teaching of sexology to master's degree psychology students and for South African Medical Association master's programmes in Family Practice has always been from a transparently biblical perspective. This has inspired several professionals to drop their secular models in a favour of a more soundly biblical approach. My ongoing medical practice, my position as Maritime and Consular doctor for the Italian Consulate in Cape Town, publication of more than two dozen professional journal articles, consulting editorship for three journals, radio and television debates in South Africa and abroad have all provided a public profile. All this has resulted in scores of opportunities to challenge non-Christian authorities and influential liberal Christian bodies who deny the inspiration and sufficiency of Scripture, Christ's deity or the gospel.

As Registrar and National Executive member of the Church of England in South Africa, and as a local church elder, a passion for sound expository preaching, church planting and youth work was nurtured. Testimonies that continue to reach me today are a humbling reminder of God's mercy in using my denomination to reach so many people of all races through church plants, camps, seminars, retreats, sermons and Bible studies.

A politically inspired terrorist attack on my church, which left a dozen people dead and nearly 50 wounded, led to a ministry in post-traumatic stress disorder and acute trauma counselling. This kind of counselling has been used many times in the violent socio-political climate that persists in South Africa today, as well as in natural disaster and accident situations.

When called on by the South African government to give expert witness during the transition from pre- to post-apartheid rule, opportunities arose for me to present legislators with Christian models and practical solutions to issues such as homosexual rights, pornography control and abortion. It is gratifying to find influential public figures today still expounding and implementing the biblical models they embraced then.

My ongoing relationship with CWR led to me going to Sri Lanka, and Malaysia and Singapore in the late 1990s to hold counselling seminars. That introduction to Asian culture has resulted in me making several visits since. Seminars in churches and radio work brought invitations to consult with Singaporean government departments tasked with developing sexuality education programmes. In contrast with the West, Asian communities have in the past been reticent to discuss sexual issues at school and at home. Catapulted by technology into a sexually explicit global village, they are now seeking answers, and have found the morally sound and cutting edge professional balance I could offer them very appealing.

I have been involved in joint projects with CWR, including the production of written, audio and video material, as well as helping in some measure with the development of joint counselling programmes with London Bible College and the first Principles of Biblical Counselling course. I have presented Principles of Biblical Counselling and Learning to Care courses, modified to suit my teaching style and South African audiences, for many years.

Dozens of seminars in all continents have followed that early CWR training, but always its influence remains evident. CWR has undoubtedly reshaped my professional thinking and, together with my evangelical training, has opened the door to many opportunities for me to reach and help change many people with a vibrant biblical alternative to the darkness of this fallen world, from academia to the corridors of power and the home. WAH planted seeds that, in spite of our imperfect selves, through sheer grace have borne a crop of saved souls around the world.

Soli deo Gloria!

SPEAKING
WITHOUT SHAKING!

Camilla Douglas

Attending a CWR Institute in Christian Counselling course has led graduates in many directions. The course helped Camilla Douglas to take the step of faith to become involved in the support of parents through her work with Positive Parenting. Camilla and her husband, Malcolm, have three children themselves – now all grown up. They attend Basingstoke Community Church.

Malcolm and I became Christians soon after we were married 30 years ago. I had never given any serious thought to Christianity before then. However, once challenged with the facts of the gospel I began to think deeply about my life and where it was going. If God really loved me and had a plan for my life it made sense to give my life back to Him. It's a decision I have never regretted.

For the first 20 years of married life I was happily involved with my family. However, without realising it, I had got into a bit of a rut. My Christian life was boring and I was living well within my 'comfort zone'. Then my life took on a totally new direction! Several of my friends worked at CWR, including Jenny Trust (course tutor), and they often talked enthusiastically about the Institute in Christian Counselling course. I had always been interested in pastoral work, but I sensed CWR was approaching it from a totally new angle and I wanted to find out more. I applied to attend the 1991–92 course with a certain amount of trepidation, not having done any academic work for years.

Although I had no obvious problems I could put my finger on, the fact that I suffered from constant low-level anxiety indicated (to any good ICC student) that all was not well within! I couldn't stand at the front and speak without shaking, found it impossible to say 'No' to a request, and was unwilling to take risks. Coming to grips with a misplaced dependency was one of the most difficult, but worthwhile, journeys I have taken. It freed me to be willing and able to pursue a totally new path of Christian service. That path would have been too daunting to embark upon without the ministry and help I had received through CWR.

After finishing the ICC course I met a remarkable woman called Eileen Jones, who founded Positive Parenting. In true pioneering spirit, Eileen invited me to get involved with the work. Positive Parenting is a national charity with over 25 years' experience in support of the family. The vision is to see training and support accessible to all parents within their local community. The organisation's main activities are publishing, training and community parenting programmes.

Positive Parenting offers a choice of parenting programmes. Time Out for Parents! is a basic course for mums and dads with children aged 0–10. Time Out for Special Needs is for parents of youngsters with particular needs. We also have a course designed especially for fathers. The courses reflect CWR's influence in that they contain simplified elements of the Institute in Christian Counselling course. We have a nationwide training programme available for those wishing to run courses.

My work involves creating new resources and – I laugh as I think about it – a great deal of public speaking. I really enjoy this now – without shaking! My other area of work is helping to establish a national network of trained course facilitators to run workshops and courses in their local community. Over the last few years we have been able to help over 3,000 parents and teams are now springing up all over the country. We are always interested to hear of others who might like to join the network.

Parenting groups are a great way of sharing ideas and experiences. All parents at some stage find themselves asking questions like 'Am I doing OK as a parent?', 'Is my child's behaviour normal?' and 'How do other parents cope?' We would love to see parenting support available in all mums and toddler groups, schools and community groups as a regular part of life, so that these kinds of questions can be answered and parents' confidence increased.

I thank God for leading me to do the Institute in Christian Counselling course. Without Him dealing with me during that course I would not have been able to become involved in the exciting and fruitful work of Positive Parenting.

FRUIT-BEARING THROUGH THE PAIN

Daphne Cox

Helping hurting people is a major part of CWR's ministry. Daphne Cox, who became a Director in 1995, knows much about this, both on a professional and a personal level. She has spent much of her life as a nurse, not only on hospital wards, but also as a hospice sister in Sydenham, London, running another hospice in Bath and, with her husband, Bryan, as a warden of flats for the elderly they established in Teignmouth. Bryan was diagnosed as having motor neurone disease in 1992 and went to be with the Lord the following March. Before that devastating diagnosis, Daphne and Bryan had been hosts to CWR courses at Waverley – something that Daphne continued to do after Bryan's passing. She has also arranged CWR courses through her local church in Winsley, Wiltshire, and is a local magistrate.

My Christian parents dedicated me as a baby at a Baptist church. We often had preachers and missionaries to lunch and tea and I always had to be quiet so that my parents could rest! I was always keen at doing well in Sunday school and at 14 was converted during a baptismal service. I had heard Billy Graham as a child and later on helped out behind the scenes at his meetings in Manchester.

Three years later I started training to be a nurse – a career that lasted until 1996 when I was forced to retire with osteoarthritis of my spine. During those years I was a staff nurse, ward sister, district nurse, community health nurse tutor, hospice director and warden to old people's flats. I finished nursing doing what I loved best: working with patients and families at home.

My parents, who were elderly even when I was born, died in a five-year period in the 1960s, as did the third person I was living with – my 95-year-old grandmother. I felt that all my earthly props had been removed and I knew I had to be totally reliant on the Lord. I then had an encounter with the Holy Spirit and from that day onwards the Lord had my full commitment.

In 1989 my sister, who was 14 years older than me, died in her 50s.

I was 41 when I married Bryan. We declared at our wedding that 'As for me and my household, we will serve the LORD' (Josh. 24:15). We loved reading the Scriptures together. We started using *Every Day with Jesus* around 1985 and gained so much from it. This really was the start of my involvement with CWR's ministry, for advertised in one issue of *EDWJ* was a Basic Biblical Counselling course (which went through many changes and was renamed Institute in Christian Counselling) at Fairmile Court. I did not find the course easy, but subsequently came to realise what valuable insights I gained from it.

In August 1988 Bryan and I became CWR Partners and started coming to Waverley Abbey House for weekends. We felt very much part of the family there. At the end of one such weekend we were asked if we would consider becoming course hosts. I immediately said 'Yes!' Bryan was happy, too, although he had sometimes been desperately tired at the end of a working week and I had wondered whether I should be dragging him to Waverley for a weekend. But I would say, 'You will feel better when you are there.' And he did.

We often spent several days and weekends at Waverley on hosting duties and after Bryan's passing I carried on with this. I have hosted and attended over 30 different courses, including Dynamic Christian Living, a lot on counselling and ministry to women.

Bryan's condition deteriorated in spring 1992 and in November, by which time he could hardly walk, he was diagnosed as having motor neurone disease. On the way home from hospital to face the future not knowing how much time we had left together, Bryan was already looking forward to seeing his twin sister, who had died of lung cancer 18 months previously. Questions about the progress of the disease tumbled out, including 'Will I waste away?' Bryan knew I had nursed motor neurone sufferers at a hospice.

The whole evangelical Anglican church we belonged to was stunned. The rector asked everyone to pray for us and so many people came to our house in response that they overflowed from the lounge into an adjoining room and up the stairs. The rector laid hands on both of us and anointed us with oil. A small group continued to meet with us for prayer. Many others came individually to pray.

Bryan found great encouragement in Isaiah 53, 'Surely he took up our infirmities …' (to which Bryan would add, 'and that includes motor neurone disease') '… and by his wounds we are healed' (NIV). Another scripture was Job 42:12, 'The LORD blessed the latter part of Job's life more than the first.' We prayed that through this illness the Lord's name would be glorified until Bryan's healing.

I took Bryan to church on as many Sundays as he was able to manage in a wheelchair. One Sunday, the last time he was on the Bible passage reading rota, I wheeled him to the front of the church where, with failing breath, he thanked the congregation for all their support and prayers. Many still remember that, helped by the Bibles I subsequently bought for every pew in his memory. As I hear the rustle of pages each Sunday I know this would delight his heart.

Bryan deteriorated rapidly and 16 weeks after the diagnosis was incapable of doing anything for himself. I was able to nurse him right up to the moment he died peacefully at home at the age of 58. Right up to his home-call he worked for missionaries, dictating to me what should be done about insurance for individuals and societies. His GP described him as a shining vision and an example of how Christians should face death.

I dreamt about Bryan not long after he died, although more likely it was a vision. I saw him walking away from me, waving. He looked more 'normal' than when I had last seen him physically. The Lord had indeed healed him in His own way and in His own time.

The Bible says that unless a seed of wheat falls to the ground and dies it will not bear fruit (John 12:24). The group that had met with us for prayer and fellowship during Bryan's illness continued for a while after Bryan's death and we all became very close to each other. We disbanded when the church started Alpha courses. All of us became group leaders and I administered the courses for six years. When the first Alpha group wanted to do an outreach I arranged for Jeannette

Barwick to come over from Waverley to speak on Being a Secure Woman. Nearly 200 ladies attended. Other CWR speakers have come to the church. Beverley Shepherd spoke one Saturday morning about Women in the Workplace and Wanda Nash led a weekend seminar on dealing with stress.

After retiring from nursing in 1996 I had a burden for ongoing biblically-based training for new Christians in our church. So I started a Friday morning group for ladies, which is affectionately known as The Friday Girls. We have seen tremendous answers to prayer, including intercession for unsaved husbands. One young father had an amazing conversion recently. The group meets at my house even when I am away and use *Every Day with Jesus* and the new *Inspiring Women Every Day*. They really appreciate this ministry.

Having trained as a Lay Pastoral Assistant, I lead the pastoral team at my village church and am also responsible for the prayer ministry.

I became a CWR Director in 1995 after the Lord had confirmed that this was what He wanted me to do through 2 Corinthians 12:9 – 'My grace is sufficient for you, for my power is made perfect in weakness.' Without that I would have felt inadequate for the task. So nowadays my main activities at Waverley are attending Board meetings and being a member of the Ladies' weekends team, something I have done for a number of years. It is wonderful to see how those who attend these weekends go home richly blessed and eager to come back for more!

I have been a local magistrate for over ten years and I also have had opportunities to speak about the hospice movement, when I was able to include my testimony, especially to the fact that I could not have done this work without God's help. When I was a sister at St Christopher's Hospice in Sydenham, southeast London, working closely with Dame Cicely Saunders (founder of the modern-day hospice movement), I knelt each morning and evening on the ward and prayed with the patients there.

Something else I do is to provide bed and breakfast for some doctors doing their GP training. Their tutor is a friend and former colleague. This allows the doctors to live in the area and be available on call. I kept in touch with them after they left and they now have eight children between them. They are a kind of extended family. Closer family connections are three granddaughters who live locally, so I am very blessed. And despite the loss of Bryan, my parents, sister and grandmother, I rejoice that they were all the Lord's children and are dwelling with Him.

MARRIAGE AND
A NEW MINISTRY

Varujan & Emma Smallwood

Joining CWR as youth project workers led to marriage for Varujan and Emma Smallwood and to the setting up of Educate, an organisation dedicated to evangelising and discipling young people in schools. The experience they gained through involvement with the WAY (Waverley Abbey Youth), helping to write and edit YP's (Young People's Every Day with Jesus) and the insights gained on the one-year Institute in Biblical Studies course are the foundation stones on which their present ministry is being built up.

It was through using *Young People's Every Day with Jesus* that I (Emma) first came into contact with CWR, having grown up in a Christian family and being involved in Church life since I was young. At 12 I came to know Jesus as my personal Saviour. *YP's* helped me to get to know the Bible. Var's first contact with CWR was through a short spell of working in the kitchen. From a non-Christian family, he became a Christian at 23 when he was a drama student. *Every Day with Jesus* helped him grow in his new-found faith. He became a member of Esher Green Baptist Church and after we were married it became home church for both of us. Var is an elder and, as he's soon to finish his theology degree at Spurgeon's College, has a regular preaching slot. I play drums in the worship team.

We both joined CWR in September 1994 as youth workers, assisting Mick Brooks in the WAY. A vision for this project at that time was to use woodland next to Waverley Abbey House for youth camps and other young people's activities, but eventually we found that it was best to focus our evangelism efforts through visiting primary and secondary schools in the area. We took assemblies and RE lessons in many of the latter, while in primary schools we did three children's plays we had both written. We also worked closely with local church youth leaders and ran outreach events called Insite.

Mick was *YP's* editor when we joined CWR, so we began to write articles and do interviews for this publication. When Mick's role changed we took over some of the editing and wrote the middle section, which we called, guess what, Insite! We carried on writing and editing *YP's* and the *YP's* website even after we left CWR in 1997 before finally giving it up in 2001. Since then I have written a children's holiday club resource for CWR, called *Mission: Miracle Maker*, with Jeni Wilson, an Educate colleague.

In many ways it's not surprising that we ended up married to each other, especially after spending the first year sharing a very small office! Our happy day was in 1996.

Being at CWR proved a key time for us – not just because we met and married! We'd both had previous experience of working with Christian organisations. I had trained with Youth for Christ on their Operation Gideon scheme and Var had worked with Riding Lights Theatre Company, so we both found working with everyone at CWR a natural progression. Because the WAY was a new venture we were able to shape and develop our work, with Mick's help, in the direction we felt it would work best. This was both exciting and challenging, not least because neither of us had experience of building a ministry from scratch before. Right from the start we were learning new skills and working with a wide cross section of people.

CWR gave us plenty of support and we had many exciting opportunities to develop our ministry, both individually and together. Our time at Waverley was definitely the launch pad for what we do now. Our ministry in schools taught us new communication and presentation skills as well as how to interact more effectively with young people and staff. We had lots of opportunities to write new materials for use in schools and churches, as well as acquiring skills through writing for *YP's*. The staff at CWR gave us much encouragement in what we were doing, some of them being mad enough to be in the children's plays we toured the primary schools with!

Early in 1997 we began to feel that our time at CWR was coming to an end, but we didn't know what to do next. When we married we had moved to Hersham, Surrey, and got quite involved with the Esher Green Church ministry, so more and more we felt that if we were going to do schools work we needed to be involved in it nearer to home. Then it would be easier to form long-term relationships with pupils and staff. After lots of prayer and a talking with friends and colleagues, we felt God was leading us to set up our own schools ministry in Hersham. CWR was totally behind us and helped to get Educate up and running.

Educate is a Christian charity working in north Surrey. When it first started it was just the two of us working from our little flat. A group of friends became trustees and at the end of 1997 we gained charitable status. The aim of Educate is to evangelise and disciple young people in schools and we adapt our methods of doing this as we go along. The work has grown and we now have four full-time workers operating from a little office in the Theatre in Leatherhead. We take assemblies and RE lessons in secondary schools and run after-school clubs. Schools have Relational Youth Workers as part of the pastoral set-up and we're there to be a friend to pupils and, where needed, provide a listening ear or a shoulder to cry on. We're not official counsellors, but sometimes we do help students during lesson times.

One thing we wanted to do right from the start was to work with other churches and especially link-up with youth workers. God has blessed us with very good links with fellowships and we regularly work with youth workers in the area. Once a year we run a residential event called Destiny, which is supported by 11 churches. Young people we meet in schools are invited to come along to this and for three days they take part in lots of crazy fun activities. They also have a chance to respond to the gospel. Over 200 of them aged 11–18 have come along.

In 1999 we moved home to the council estate in Esher and got involved with the community there. The Educate team started a youth club and it has been going ever since!

Taking part in the one-year Institute in Biblical Studies course at Waverley was foundational for what we do now. Under the expert tuition of Phil Greenslade, we began to understand the amazing story of salvation in the Bible. The course opened up a whole new way of reading and interpreting the Scriptures for us and almost immediately we began to take what we had been taught and adapt it for the young people we were teaching.

We've both done further theology study, but the IBS teaching has probably had the biggest impact on our lives. We've been able to use what we have learned at CWR in so many ways and, no doubt, will continue to do so.

GETTING REAL

Roselyn Abbott

Having come to Waverley as a one-year Institute in Biblical Studies student, Roselyn Abbott returned the following year for the one-year Institute in Christian Counselling. She subsequently became a CWR counselling course tutor before leaving to concentrate on developing Get Real! – a pastoral discipleship course run in Southampton and based on the CWR model of Christian counselling.

I came to Waverley in September 1993 hoping to spend two years in study retreat. I believed that I had irretrievably ruined my life and Christian ministry through adultery and needed to experience God's forgiveness and restoration. The one-year Institute in Biblical Studies took me a long way down the road towards that restoration, making a deep impact on me. After the course was finished my hope of a second year of studying at Waverley was realised when I was accepted for the Institute in Christian Counselling course.

I found that God ministered to me very directly at Waverley and experienced first hand what seems to be His anointing on the very fabric of the building. The Lord spoke to me mainly about who I was and what He was calling me to do. A lot of it was focused around the life of Moses, including my identifying with his difficulty in being able to speak fluently! Essentially, Father God was speaking to me about the deliverance and restoration of the Bride of Christ and my part in that process. This was confirmed to me when Selwyn Hughes spoke at our ICC prizegiving in 1995 about a great wave of destiny coming over all in the room.

Not long afterwards I was back at Waverley as a course tutor on the one-year and modular ICC. I had co-written some material for a similar course for Central Counselling Service in Southampton and, as a consequence, CWR invited me to teach on their own counselling programme. After a year or so I left to focus on family concerns, concentrate on my work at Community Church Southampton and especially to develop Get Real!

Get Real! stemmed from a therapy group called *ruah* that I usually run annually. In 1997–98 I had adapted the CWR model for use in this group and was then invited by Allan Cox at Community Church Southampton to set it in the pastoral context for discipleship groups. So Get Real! was born. Now it is run twice annually at Community Church and at least three times a year in other churches in the South of England. We also run one-off taster days and have piloted a youth course and a course adapted for adults with special needs. During 2002 nearly 500 people attended Get Real! in one form or another. The Get Real! textbook, to which Selwyn has contributed a very encouraging foreword, is due to be published during 2003.

The pathway leading to my ministry of starting and developing Get Real! has taken many twists and turns and I thank the Lord for His love, grace and faithfulness in removing all the stones. I became a Christian at 11 when being confirmed as a Roman Catholic. The bishop suggested that we might like to invite Jesus into our hearts. I did. But I wasn't thoroughly discipled until I was 27, after I had travelled all round the spiritual houses from Roman Catholicism to New Age and the occult. I joined Blandford Evangelical Church in Dorset and was baptised. In 1996 my husband, Richard, our son and daughter (now in their late teens) and I moved to Southampton and I became involved in counselling work at Community Church. I am also a member of Testwood Baptist Church, where our family worships.

As well as working on Get Real! I have also been involved with Central Counselling Service as an individual and group counsellor, supervisor and counselling trainer, and offer private counselling practice in those areas. On top of all this I am studying analytic group work at the Department of Psychiatry, Royal South Hants Hospital, and hope to do further studies.

My first contact with CWR was through using *Every Day with Jesus*, which I found thought provoking and challenging, as well as encouraging me to read the Scriptures every day. Then in 1992 I attended a three-week Institute in Christian Counselling course and a one-day Helping the Homosexual seminar – useful introductions to the years I spent studying and teaching at Waverley. Get Real! is both the fulfilment of what God spoke to me about there and the practical outworking of all that I have learned from CWR.

CALLED TO COUNSEL
THE POLICE!

Olivia Kyambadde

Through attending a three-week Institute in Christian Counselling course at Waverley, Olivia Kyambadde returned home to start a counselling ministry in one of Uganda's fastest growing churches – the 8,000-strong Kampala Pentecostal Church. In 2001 God led her into counselling police officers at their training school. Olivia is married to Jenner, a banker, and they have four children of their own and three adopted children of deceased brothers and sisters.

CWR's ministry has been a great help to me over the years. Through using *Every Day with Jesus* in my devotionals I found out about a three-week Institute in Christian Counselling course and came to England in 1993 to attend it. I had, for some time before that, realised God was calling me to a counselling ministry and those three weeks at Waverley gave me the necessary skills – and polished me up! The course helped me to be real, to understand and accept myself for who I really am. I was taught by people who did not have any masks and this enabled me to begin to get rid of the masks I was wearing.

When I returned home I shared my dream about starting a counselling ministry with the senior pastor of Kampala Pentecostal Church, Gary Skinner. He gave me a room in the church. It had no furniture, but we obtained what we needed at very low cost as a result of my husband's company, Shell Uganda, selling off old items. In July 2002 Angie Coombes and Nicky-Sue Leonard came to the church to hold counsellor training sessions for pastors and ministry leaders. These leaders thought they were attending to acquire counselling skills but were amazed to find that they themselves were being counselled. The result was that they opened up their lives for the Lord to change them. They were healed of past hurts and began to look at counselling from a new perspective.

Kampala Pentecostal Church is one of the fastest growing churches in Uganda. It is a cell-based church with about 8,000 members and is divided into five districts. A pastor leads each district and it has youth, children's and missions' leaders. Two years ago a satellite church was started. KPC also has a ministry to orphans. Most of these youngsters lost their parents through the AIDS scourge. Called the Watoto Child Care ministry, it has 55 units in three homes. In each unit a housemother looks after eight children. In addition, there are also 800 children being cared for in extended families. The ministry also runs schools for these children.

It was during a time of personal crisis that God opened up the way for me to counsel Uganda's police and train officers to become counsellors. One night in 2001 I was praying for direction. We had gone through a lot of trials as a family and were really wondering what God had in store for us. Having lost everything we owned, including homes, businesses and other property, it felt as if we did not have a private life any more. I had returned from Haggai Institute leadership training in Singapore, where we had been challenged to do something that only God could bring about, but here I was feeling lost and confused. As I prayed, however, I felt the Holy Spirit speaking to me and instructing me to work with the Uganda police force.

I almost jumped out of bed because that was something I would never have thought about. The police!

But as these thoughts raced through my mind I remembered that the force had just gone through a judicial inquiry in which it had been ridiculed and left feeling very ashamed. I felt the Holy Spirit tell me that they needed someone to understand them, to help them pick up the pieces and become an efficient force for justice. I also felt the Spirit say that God wanted to work through the dejected police force to demonstrate His love and power to the people of Uganda. He chose me because He had prepared me and, being a counsellor, He wanted me to go and use my skills to counsel them with His love and compassion.

I asked God for a sign. I said that if this was really from Him I should hear something about the police the following morning. I shared this with my husband and we both waited to see what God would do. In the morning Jenner brought me the daily newspaper. On the front page was a large photograph of the Inspector General of Police. I knew I was really in business with God.

I went to the police headquarters and met the man himself. I presented the idea of working with him to redeem the image of the police in the eyes of the public. He was very receptive and introduced me to the officer in charge of training. This led to me being able to hold group counselling sessions at the police training school and counselling was incorporated into the syllabus. Each student goes through one-to-one counselling.

I have seen these officers being transformed through these sessions. Most of them are unwilling to start with, but end up wanting more and more. It is wonderful to see God touching them and encouraging them.

I became a Christian during my second year at secondary school through Scripture Union Bible study groups. Although I had always believed that I was a good girl, doing things to the best of my ability, careful not to tread on people's toes and being a joy to my parents, I came to realise that I could never please God with good deeds. I was still a sinner and I needed Jesus who died for me. I thank God for His Son and for leading me into His service as a counsellor. In His perfect will and purposes, my training at Waverley has had a good deal to do with that!

SAVED THROUGH
SELWYN'S MINISTRY

Nigel James

One March evening in 1982 Selwyn Hughes was leading a New Life for Sussex Crusade meeting at The Dome, Brighton, with a local evangelist. One of those who came to the front to be prayed for and give his life to Jesus Christ was Nigel James. Today Nigel is Counselling Training Co-ordinator at Waverley Abbey House.

I had been seeking and searching for God and the answers to life for quite a while before that life-changing meeting at The Dome, Brighton, on 14 March 1982. I was in a well-paid job and enjoying all the material trappings of business success within the photographic industry. But one of my customers, Derek Moon, often talked to me gently about Christian matters and I found myself pondering over what he said. Then my ex-wife's sister-in-law invited me to a guest service at Bishop Hannington Anglican church in Hove. There the vicar and his wife encouraged me to attend the mission at The Dome.

Everything said on the first night there seemed to speak to me personally and answered many of the questions I had been asking. I went back there on the next four nights. On the last night, to my astonishment, I saw Derek Moon on the stage playing the electric organ. When the appeal came for those who wanted to give their lives to Jesus to go forward, I ran to the front to be prayed for by Derek, Selwyn and Mike Sprenger, a Brighton-based evangelist. The feeling I experienced as I asked the Lord Jesus to take over my life was amazing.

Soon afterwards I met Jan, who had been a Christian for a long time and, like myself, had gone through the trauma of divorce. We were married in 1986.

Back at my work as marketing director of a photographic trade processing laboratory, I gradually seemed to be more and more involved in helping staff with their personal problems. As Jan also had pastoral gifts, we decided to attend the CWR Caring Seminars at Hove Town Hall. During those seminars Selwyn mentioned plans to hold a new one-year counselling course at Waverley Abbey House, starting in 1988 or '89. We expressed our interest and details were subsequently sent to us. I had a strong sense that God was saying I should attend, although I had no idea why.

The only problem about attending this course was my job. But trusting in the Lord I approached the company's managing director to ask whether he would release me to attend a Christian counselling course every Monday during term-time. He was not a believer, but simply said 'Fine!' But there was another problem: the course was due to start in the autumn, which was difficult because of the amount of work I had to do during this busy period. Then there was a postal strike, which delayed the applications and responses from potential students. So CWR put back the start of the course until January 1989. This was ideal for me (and others, it transpired).

On the first day of the course I found myself sitting next to my ex-wife's sister-in-law! She told me she had been praying hard for me to give my life to the Lord. Selwyn was surprised, too, and delighted, to discover that one of the people he had prayed for at The Dome nearly seven years earlier was sitting in front of him at the first one-year Institute in Christian Counselling course.

The ICC course was life-changing, causing me to grow in my relationship with Jesus, giving me a new awareness of how to apply His teaching to daily living and developing pastoral care gifts.

In 1990 Phil Greenslade launched the one-year Institute in Biblical Studies and I was among several of the first ICC students who joined this challenging course. Meanwhile, my managing director, who had agreed to release me for a second year of CWR studies, announced that he was selling the business to go into hot air ballooning. The company that took over asset-stripped the laboratory and made everyone over a certain age and salary redundant – including me.

I was left wondering what to do, but then CWR asked if I would like to join the staff to help with counselling training administration. John Wright, a dear man whom I had come to know while on the courses, was due to retire at the end of the year and it was planned that I should spend three months with him from September to pick up the reins. I was on holiday that August when CWR phoned with the very sad news that John had died suddenly from a heart attack. But could I start anyway? I did so, working with Jeannette Barwick in what was then the Counselling Centre, as well as helping Jenny Trust one day a week on the one-year ICC course.

I became increasingly involved with CWR's counselling courses over the next three years, mainly with administration, applicant screening and as a facilitator. In the mid 1990s I helped Paul Grant set up and run the counselling element of the theology and counselling course in partnership with London

Bible College. When Paul retired in July 2001 I became Counselling Training Co-ordinator. Today I work at Waverley three days a week, sometimes four. I enjoy the work immensely; probably because I've known most of the people we work with for quite a number of years. Many of our lecturers and presenters were originally students on the year-long courses and, like me, have been impacted deeply by the teaching and especially the model of counselling developed by Selwyn.

Both Jan and I have grown-up children from our previous marriages and also Tom, our teenage son. We have seen the hand of God upon him, for after much prayer he has been healed of the distressing bowel abnormality he was born with. We belong to Cowfold Christian Fellowship, one of the New Frontiers group of churches. Jan and I have been involved with Alpha, leading homegroups and nurture groups for new Christians. My experience in leading groups and pastoral work at Waverley has been invaluable.

The Lord's hand has been very evident on my life, especially over the past 20 years. He has put the right people in my path at key stages of the journey – not least Selwyn in my conversion and subsequent involvement at Waverley.

THE WEEK THAT CHANGED ME

Lynn Penson

A week-long counselling course at Waverley Abbey House was the turning point for Lynn Penson. It has not only transformed her life but impacted many students she has taught and counselled at Moorlands College at Sopley, Christchurch. Lynn is married to Andrew, a civil engineer, who has also been involved with the Moorlands ministry. They have a daughter and two sons. Their elder son, aged 17, has been diagnosed ADHD and dyspraxic. As well as being a Church history tutor at Moorlands, Lynn is at present studying for a MTh degree at Spurgeon's College part-time. She and her family are members of Cranleigh Community Church near their home in Bournemouth.

I was brought up in a home with a strong Christian influence. My father pioneered an Assemblies of God church in Cwmbran, South Wales, and was its pastor for many years. I grew up with a love of the things of God and made a commitment to follow Christ very early in life. A key point in my Christian experience was listening to a youth evangelist, Brian Downward, preaching on the parable of the two sons, focusing on the son who did not go away. God wonderfully spoke to me to the effect that I did not need to go and experience worldly ways to make my testimony valid – He wanted to keep me from those things. I was only about 12 or 13 at the time, but here I was listening to a man confirming the things that God had spoken directly to me earlier that day.

I gained a theology degree at Leeds University and became a

schoolteacher. Moving to the Bournemouth area, Andrew and I found ourselves in the same house group as Brian Butler, then Vice-Principal of Moorlands College. Because of my degree he asked me to do a series of lectures for local Christians on ethical issues. This led to teaching on Church history, ethics and communication at the college. I returned to school teaching for several years but today I am back at Moorlands lecturing part-time on Church history. Andrew has been administrator and bursar at the college, so it was our life and ministry for a number of years even though I have never been a full-time tutor there.

It was through lecturing at Moorlands College that I came into contact with CWR. In 1990 I was the only female tutor at Moorlands and found myself increasingly involved in pastoral care of the women students. I often found myself out of depth in this. I was able to listen and empathise but felt ill equipped to help people move on. So it was suggested that I attend a course at CWR. Another staff member found it useful, so it seemed like a good idea.

I went to Waverley Abbey House expecting to pick up a few useful techniques. I came back a changed person!

During that week-long Introduction to Christian Counselling course in September 1990 everything about me was put under the spotlight. It was as if, like an onion, all the layers were being peeled away. Everything we did on the course challenged me. I shall never forget the tears that would not stop running down my cheeks as Selwyn Hughes spoke about where we find our security, self-worth and significance. I realised how

I had used my role at Bible college to give myself a sense of significance and worth. I needed the job more than it needed me! If I had lost it I would have felt worthless. Yet I was struggling with it, feeling ill every morning before lecturing: What if I got it wrong? What if someone asked me a question I did not know the answer to? What if they didn't like me? I loved what I was doing, but at the same time it terrified me!

I also realised the burden I was putting on my husband to provide me with security. I could not accept that he simply loved me – or that anyone else could, for that matter. I found it hard to accept praise and appreciation from him, colleagues or students.

By the penultimate day at Waverley I was feeling very vulnerable, that my whole life was in shreds. Yet God wonderfully put me back together again – a new model this time! On *the* last night I lay in bed hardly able to sleep. The chorus *I am a new creation* kept playing through my mind. It summed everything up: though I had long been God's child, He was doing something new in my life.

I understood, really for the first time, His unconditional love and acceptance. I had known it in my head, and even spoken about it, but it had now become reality. I understood my worth to God not only for what I did but also for who I am, that it was not through anything I did but through His grace. The joy that came with this understanding was immense. My personal Christian walk was transformed and since then I have enjoyed the fact that God delights in me! I realised that I did not have to fear God and feel guilty that I could not attain the standards I had set myself. He was lovingly with me as I continued on my journey of being transformed into His likeness.

After returning home I found my encounter with God began to change my family life, as I no longer looked to my husband constantly for affirmation. It took an enormous burden off him.

I love the CWR model of looking at the whole person. After that course I found that even my personal Bible studies were different as I considered the wider impact of an encounter with Jesus on the lives of those we read about in the Scriptures.

In 1991 I went back to Waverley for a Continuation Course in Christian Counselling and built on the benefits I had previously received. I have used the insights constantly in pastoral situations, especially with Bible college students and their wives. Many people have benefited from what I learned at Waverley.

Andrew and I attended a Marriage Enrichment weekend at Waverley, which not only reaffirmed and strengthened our own marriage, but also led to us hosting weekends at Moorlands for married students. When Dave and Joyce Ames returned to America after many years of leading such seminars in Britain, we replaced them for this annual seminar, which we call Marriage on Track. The response has been encouraging and we have also been able to minister further in this area through attending CWR's Caring for Troubled Marriages and Preparing People for Marriage seminars.

My personal work with students and their wives or husbands has expanded. I have seen so many people come to train to serve the Lord yet struggle in their relationship with Him and with others. It has been such a privilege to get alongside some of these students, who are now Church leaders, and encourage them to discover who they are in Christ, knowing that this would equip them better in their ministries.

God has worked powerfully on my life since September 1990 at Waverley and this has had an impact on everything I do. My lecturing, preaching, teaching, leading of retreats inside and outside Moorlands, quiet days and pastoral counselling all flow out of God's transforming work during that week. When I lecture it is no longer with the gripping fear of getting it wrong. This releases me to teach with all the passion I have for my subject. When I preach it is in the security of God's love, whatever the response from the congregation. When I talk to someone who cannot appreciate God's love for them I do so in the light of the transformation He has brought to my own understanding and relationship with Him.

National Distributors

UK: (and countries not listed below)
CWR, Waverley Abbey House, Waverley Lane, Farnham, Surrey GU9 8EP.
Tel: (01252) 784700 Outside UK (44) 1252 784700

AUSTRALIA: CMC Australasia, PO Box 519, Belmont, Victoria 3216.
Tel: (03) 5241 3288

CANADA: Cook Communications Ministries, PO Box 98, 55 Woodslee Avenue,
Paris, Ontario. Tel: 1800 263 2664

GHANA: Challenge Enterprises of Ghana, PO Box 5723, Accra.
Tel: (021) 222437/223249 Fax: (021) 226227

HONG KONG: Cross Communications Ltd, 1/F, 562A Nathan Road, Kowloon.
Tel: 2780 1188 Fax: 2770 6229

INDIA: Crystal Communications, 10-3-18/4/1, East Marredpally, Secunderabad
– 500 026. Tel/Fax: (040) 7732801

KENYA: Keswick Books and Gifts Ltd, PO Box 10242, Nairobi.
Tel: (02) 331692/226047 Fax: (02) 728557

MALAYSIA: Salvation Book Centre (M) Sdn Bhd, 23 Jalan SS 2/64, 47300
Petaling Jaya, Selangor. Tel: (03) 78766411/78766797
Fax: (03) 78757066/78756360

NEW ZEALAND: CMC Australasia, PO Box 36015, Lower Hutt.
Tel: 0800 449 408 Fax: 0800 449 049

NIGERIA: FBFM, Helen Baugh House, 96 St Finbarr's College Road, Akoka,
Lagos. Tel: (01) 7747429/4700218/825775/827264

PHILIPPINES: OMF Literature Inc, 776 Boni Avenue, Mandaluyong City.
Tel: (02) 531 2183 Fax: (02) 531 1960

REPUBLIC OF IRELAND: Scripture Union, 40 Talbot Street, Dublin 1.
Tel: (01) 8363764

SINGAPORE: Armour Publishing Pte Ltd, Block 203A Henderson Road,
11–06 Henderson Industrial Park, Singapore 159546. Tel: 6 276 9976
Fax: 6 276 7564

SOUTH AFRICA: Struik Christian Books, 80 MacKenzie Street,
PO Box 1144, Cape Town 8000. Tel: (021) 462 4360 Fax: (021) 461 3612

SRI LANKA: Christombu Books, 27 Hospital Street, Colombo 1.
Tel: (01) 433142/328909

TANZANIA: CLC Christian Book Centre, PO Box 1384, Mkwepu Street, Dar es
Salaam. Tel/Fax (022) 2119439

USA: Cook Communications Ministries, PO Box 98, 55 Woodslee Avenue, Paris,
Ontario, Canada. Tel: 1800 263 2664

ZIMBABWE: Word of Life Books, Shop 4, Memorial Building,
35 S Machel Avenue, Harare. Tel: (04) 781305 Fax: (04) 774739

For email addresses, visit the CWR website: www.cwr.org.uk
CWR is a registered charity – number 294387

Trusted
All Over the World

Daily Devotionals

    Books and Videos

Day and Residential Courses

    Counselling Training

Biblical Study Courses

    Regional Seminars

Ministry to Women

CWR have been providing training and resources for Christians since the 1960s. From our headquarters at Waverley Abbey House we have been serving God's people with a vision to help apply God's Word to everyday life and relationships. The daily devotional *Every Day with Jesus* is read by over three-quarters of a million people in more than 150 countries, and our unique courses in biblical studies and pastoral care are respected all over the world.

For a free brochure about our seminars and courses or a catalogue of CWR resources please contact us at the following address:

**CWR,
Waverley Abbey House,
Waverley Lane,
Farnham,
Surrey GU9 8EP**

**Telephone: 01252 784700
Email: mail@cwr.org.uk
Website: www.cwr.org.uk**

Every Day with Jesus – Bimonthly

One of the most popular daily Bible study tools in the world with over three-quarters of a million readers. This inspiring devotional is available bimonthly in regular or large print and as a six-part annual subscription.

- Get practical help with life's challenges

- Gain insight into the deeper truths of Scripture

- Be challenged, comforted and encouraged

- Study six topics in depth each year

£1.95 each
£11 annual subscription
£1.95 Large Print
£11.00 Large Print annual subscription

Inspiring Women Every Day – Bimonthly

This life-enriching daily devotional written for women by women is a source of inspiration and encouragement to all ages.

£1.95 each
£11 annual subscription

- Find practical support to face the challenges of living

- Be encouraged by the insightful guidance of Scripture

- Build your faith and inspire your Christian walk with daily readings

- Features well-known writers such as Jennifer Rees Larcombe, Wendy Virgo, Helena Wilkinson, Margaret Ellis and Ali Stibbe.

Content previously published as Through the Bible Every Day in One Year

Cover to Cover

- Chronological one-year programme
- 365 undated readings – start any time of the year
- An overview of each Bible book with charts, maps, diagrams and illustrations.

£9.95 Softback book ISBN 1-85345-136-3
£9.99 Hardback book ISBN 1-85345-167-3
£9.95 6-part work Code C2CPS

God's People

- One-year programme with 58 Bible characters
- 365 undated readings – start any time of the year
- Selected readings taking approximately 10 to 15 minutes each day.

£9.95 Softback book ISBN 1-85345-160-6
£9.95 6-part work Code GPPS

Content previously published as Character by Character

God's Story

- Through the Bible promise by promise
- 365 undated readings – start any time of the year
- Daily readings reveal the relationship between the Old and New Testaments.

£9.95 Softback book ISBN 1-85345-186-X